To Jean & Peter
with every good wish

Norman & Mary

A Prospect of the West

Norman Dugdale

A PROSPECT OF THE WEST

Poems

BARRIE & JENKINS
LONDON

For my mother

A Prospect of The West

"and he a middling kind of a scarecrow, with no savagery or fine words in him at all"
J. M. Synge: The Playboy of the Western World

Contents

I

One and Many 1
Personal Appearance 2
Kerry 4
Anglican Church : West Cork 5
Two in Connemara 6
Dublin 7
Belfast 9
Persephone 11
Swift 12
Louis MacNeice 13
Lines for an Old Lady 14

II

Landfall 18
Pennines 20
Easter in Craven 21
Hawarth 22
Haven Street 24
Reasons of State 27
Downham Revisited 29
The Farther Shore 30
Tourist Season 32
Gt. Portland Street 33
Pavane for the 'Forty-Five 34
For Better for Worse 35

III

Poor Fitz	38
The Disposition of the Weather	40
Frontier Incident	42
To Venus	44
Queene and Huntresse	46
Perseus	47
Galatea to Pygmalion	48
Nocturne	49
Retrospect	51
Against Abstraction	52
An Enemy	54
A Narrow Place	55
On A Recent Happy Event	57
A Prospect of the West	58
Evensong	60
An Exorcism	63
Sea-Change	64
A Question of Identity	65
Single Ticket	67

Acknowledgements are due to the editors of the following, in which some of these poems have appeared: The Critical Survey, The Dublin Magazine, The Honest Ulsterman, The Irish Times, The Northern Review, Outposts, The Poetry Review, Phoenix, Tribune; and to The B.B.C. (North Region) and The Queen's University Festival Society.

One And Many

Lord, let me now and then forget
The bag of bones I lug round yet,
And save me from the absurd I
Who haunts these poems like a spy
In multiple disguises, shifts
That cannot hide the inner rifts.
And may I learn that good is not
Sprung elsewhere, but pitched in what,
Here and now, this common light
Reveals. So, by gifts of touch and sight
Walking my world, may I pass through
All false identities to grasp the true.

Personal Appearance

He strides in from another world, this man
Of fifty, lean survivor from
A decade out of fashion with the young
(Spain, the hunger march, the League, the pogrom).
They watch him guardedly, lest they succumb
To fame or charm, ready to detect
The slightest sleight of hand or slip of tongue.
In muddled middle-age among all these
Untouched as yet by time's perplexities,

I note the strength concealed in his repose —
Grey hair brushed back, a swarthy face, hooked nose,
Wide mouth twisting upwards at the corner,
Hands resting on his knees: the whole effect
Remarkably Roman, as of one endowed
With ruthless energy for love or war.
When he begins to speak a rasping, loud,
Commanding voice confirms the metaphor.

After the reading there is generous applause —
And yet I notice they remain unwrung
By what most moves him — then some questions, then
Leaving the warm and lighted lecture-room
We shuffle out into the mist and gloom
Of the November night. 'Frankly'—
Some golden Pyrrha, turning to her friend —
'I wasn't terribly impressed.' 'O, I don't mind
His poetry, but his teeth are yellow.'

They think of him as someone left behind,
Signalling vainly from a past now dead.
I think of him as one gone on ahead,
Deeper and deeper in the wilderness

And finding his cipher clear I realise —
Alone now, walking along streets I know —
I must have crossed the frontier long ago.

Kerry

Here Ireland thrusts a great arthritic fist
Into the green Atlantic, and a dying life
Moves with the grave slow rhythm of the waves
Expiring on tremendous beaches. Among
These bogs and stony fields, the peat-smoke
Acrid in the dusk, only the tourist
Prospers, with his camera and car
Bringing the lure of cities to the young:
Destroyer of old truth, old faith, old tongue.

Anglican Church: West Cork

A surprise, after the slap and suck of tide,
Salt spume, sun-dazzle of the estuary,
This weathered roof and spire, old spars that ride
Here in a creek of time, folded from the sea.
Drunk on foxgloves, glutted with musk-rose,
Bees weave a drowsy silence round the close.

I mark the decent plainness of squared stone:
No soaring pinnacle, arches that strain
Upwards, but measure and proportion
Resisting shake of wind, the rot of rain
Through centuries, its bulk and girth
Rooted in these few yards of racing earth.

A decent plainness too within:
No fretted vault, carved architrave,
Saints writhing in contrition of their sin
Or splendour of stained glass in choir and nave,
But seemly all, comporting with the rite,
And gathering through clear windows light.

Almost at the world's end witness to
The lucid statement of dark mysteries,
The church of Swift and Taylor, of the few
Under the nettles here and dancing bees:
The susurration of encroaching sea
All these blent voices, whispering through me.

Two In Connemara

I

This business man whose affable 'Good mornings'
Bespeak a hearty breakfast is like Crewe
Or any main-line junction thousands pass through,
Pausing only to change trains: full of smoke
And stir, announcements, rumblings,
But also useful information, comforts, things
Such as no traveller should despise —
Times of departure, destinations, tea,
Fags, paperbacks and news. Even in his guise
Of solitary fisherman he makes a crowd,
Bulky, jocular, derisive, loud.

II

The poet wears his fame as carelessly
As some old jacket baggy from long use,
Smiles, murmurs, nods to all; but being courteous
And grave by nature cannot wholly shed
The formal elegance of his address,
Transporting to the emptiness
Of bog and mountain, water, stunted wood,
His burden and his gift, the solitude
That guards his conversation with the dead.

Dublin

Autumn blusters in the square. Squalls of rain,
Scudding before a strong south-westerly
Across Kildare, spatter my window-pane
And set it rattling high above the street.
There on his pillar gull-stained Nelson drips,
Staring beyond the porter-laden Liffey
For signals from a long-since foundered fleet.

And there, investing Christ Church and St. Patrick's,
Grim forts held by a shrunken garrison,
Swarm smoky tenements, the huddled bricks
Where the city's poor lodge tight and multiply
Their kind. But shadows of the beaten dead
Stalk this town still, or crowd across its sky.
I think especially of one who fled,

The broken dreamer of a pastoral dream,
Of one out of his mind, another torn
Between his duty and desire. They seem
With Essex, Mountjoy, Wentworth, only lately gone.
Now dowagers totter in decayed hotels
Who once looked out on half a county; and wind
And rain no shutter bars or roof repels

Plunder their rooms at will and nettles grow
In houses envy gutted or their sons
Consigned to browsing cattle and the crow.
The hidden workings here of history,

Running like unmapped mines beneath the land,
Cracked the foundations, wrenched everything awry
And out of true that my kind meant to stand.

Shored-up, and fissured so, this city now
The devious Gael commands but cannot quite
Possess, embrace the queen or disavow
The harlot. To me her raddled grace,
And breath infused with whisky, stout and gin
And watery eye suggest the sort of place,
Late-rising, boozily hospitable, that might

Afford a leaky shelter now the days draw in.

Belfast

City of gull-flecked gantries, cloudy city,
Raised by steam and iron from mud and marsh,
God-ranting, canting, pious without pity,
Pillaged by gales, marauders that swarm
Out of the tempestuous Atlantic,
Trudges at daybreak, caps and dungarees
Over the bridge, wharves by sluggish water
That slops and flops its toungue against the quays,
Men in thousands moving through the murk,
Shapers of ships will cruise on cobalt seas
Elsewhere.

    Now cranes are still, clangour of steel
Suspended in the evening's sultry haze.
The smell of porter seeps through alleyways
And bits of garbage float with scum and oil,
Turning with the tide. Down reaches smooth as foil
The sirens of departing steamers
Echo from shadowy, sea-bird plaintive shores;
And slippered women issue from their doors,
Gathering at street corners with the dusk
To chat in curling-pins and aprons, call
For straying children.

    All stridency of day
The moon dissolves, revealing a blanched crone,
Confused by wrongs, troubled by old resentments,
Her memories hugged round her like a shawl,

Muttering and mumbling through the dark.
And bonfires blazing on waste lots to mark
King Billy's triumph, James's overthrow,
That cast their shifting shadows on the night
Of bogeyman and hero long ago —
Dried faggots these of ancient rancour still
Smouldering in her heart and there kept warm —

Splutter and sigh, and one by one die down;
Turn into signals of distress
By lost survivors kindled on some shore
Glitter of moon and sea's indifference drown.

Persephone

Although it cannot last,
This shock of sharp delight
The blind heart craves and chooses
That everywhere encounters you
In lanes embanked with blue
Violets and dog-roses,
These hedgerows fuchsias' flames
Run like wildfire through:

Although it cannot last,
This rock of pulse, the flush
And ripple like a race of tide
Through tranquil waters ruffling wide,
Tug of wrist divining you
In February's sleet and slush,
Among black flowers, a marguerite
Umbrellas jostle in the street:

Knowing it cannot last
Sears so; but how should this abide
Or any ecstasy
Against the rub and grin
Of the greasy world outside
Or that fault fissures all,
The sudden shift or fall
Of the fractured world within?

Swift

Dread like a storm-cloud from the start
Massed in his mind, purpled, sagged and hung
In molten menace. The slow death then of hope
Marbled him, with fleas and pygmies shut
Forever in a famished Lilliput
To suffer there the slower death of heart,
This Gulliver in chains whose monstrous head
Flashed inner lightning as the darkness spread.
To plague him still, Court flies — those clegs on dung
Each summer stirred to frantic life — buzzed their brief
Erratic dance of pomp and vanity.
Mere starving gnats that bit him till he bled
And they grew drunk upon his blood, the Irishry
As ever he despised but fed: chafed
In smoky Dublin, sodden Laracor
Under the carapace of scorn and pride
While friends fell silent, loves he had denied
Unflowered in their violated dust.

Still

The calcined heart that would not give him rest
Drove him, drove him, trudging the inchoate
Moon-cold landscape of despair
His madness lit, the crusted craters there
And choked black furnaces of his charred skull.
In slag and clinker, ashes of ancient war
Only his stumbling carcase had survived
(Whipped by serfs, battered by grief too late)

The blaze of mind went out that warmed the poor.

12

Louis MacNeice
(Buried at Carrowdore, Winter, 1963)

Alone in the keen air a hawk swings wide
Between the sea like steel and the lough's fanged shore
Of shining rock salivaed by the tide
And rakes the famished fields round Carrowdore.
Stiff yet with frost, the numbed earth hardly stirs
Through days of drought, soil's drought and drought of heart,
Ebbed season when the angry sun strikes spurs
On ice in vain or sulks in mists apart.
Soon, though, spring will come inching in, to brim
These creeks, fill silent woods with song at prime —
Mindless music he will never hear
Who over the wintry landscape of his time
Soared solitary, over the charred, grim
Stumps of cities, tundra frozen in fear.

Lines For An Old Lady

So they are all to go, then — church,
Gaunt bastion of the straitened faith
Victorian wealth and piety
Piled on these slums a century ago
To guard an Orange enclave in the Green;
The drunken alleyways that lurch
Against its sides and brawl about its feet,
Hugging their quarrel close; each crumpled street
Seething with cats by night and kids by day —
All are to go, in one great swathe
Scythed flat to make an urban motorway

And speed the suburbs into town. And this is right,
For all have served their turn and time. Now traffic's
Rising drumroll shakes the porch, flicks
Mortar loose and rumbles deep within.
The terraces like elderly bronchitics
Cough in their smoke at dawn : at nightfall wheeze,
Propped back to back and riddled with dry rot.
And phthisis eats through lungs. So let
Fire burn, bulldozers pulverise the lot —
Pews, common privies, poverty, disease,
Compounded in the dust.

                    But what then should
The unconsenting heart, itself
Grown rickety at last with age
(That rooted in blind reasons has withstood

The sour constriction of this place
And by some miracle of grace
Reaches still to light and leaf)
Do, but shrivel in such rational cold rage
To rip and batter all, and all for good?
Where else should it strike home? How put on then
The crooked glory of unlooked-for Spring
Or under its spread of memory seed again?

II

Landfall

Stiff-gaited, cumbersome, the great steel bird
Waddles to the airfield's edge, stops, suffers there
A shudder of sudden power, then lunges, lifts
And leaps, cloud-cleaving, clear into radiance,
Over the masked earth, seas and cities
Soars in seeming freedom, though curbed still,
Responsive yet to skill of hand and eye.

Despite the nubile hostess, neat in nylons,
Dispenser of charm and reassurance,
This is man's element, where risks are real
Yet calculated, the rush of chaos
Resisted by a wafer: marvellous
The thrust of mind sustaining this machine
Athwart a toppled sunset, under cold stars.

Then stoops, slithers once more through cloud. Suddenly
The city glitters in the depths below
Encrusting with innumerable jewels
The plain black velvet of the countryside.
Swings and sways above, engines cut back,
The huge wing gently scything swathes of light
While in their comfortable suburbs sit

Millions for whom the weather of the world
Is only a diagram on a screen.
So trundles to a stop on windy tarmac
Among mechanics, smells of kerosene,

Coaches, hoardings, neon-signs. We descend,
Resuming shabby lives with satisfaction
Or relief, and disperse in the wilderness

Our sharp, synoptic vision shifted, blurred
By this magnification of the night.
Earthbound, I plod parched country now,
The crumbling mass and muttering decay
Of Dis's gloomy kingdom: unredeemed unless
Some spirit singing here in time's duress
Conjures a clear spring yet beside the way.

Pennines

Mere bacilli the diesels crawl below
On twisted roads wound tight between
Smudged towns — clamped
Like crabs in the intestines of these hills.
Huddled under the smoke, a people here
With little expectation labours still:
While over the bull-necked, empty moors
In summer larksong soars, arching the silence
With intricate fan-vaulting everywhere.

Easter In Craven

East wind gnaws the fells, rubs
The white scars raw of limestone crags,
Tugs at trees, picking the skulls
Of sheep last winter knifed: nags
This northern land like toothache still.
But look, the air is luminous.
By crannied wall, crouched farmstead
First crocus thrusts, then daffodil.
The waters move beneath the earth;
The great limbs stir, tumbling bells,
Toppling gravestones, shaking the dead
In every dale. With crash of rocks,
Stiff banners blazing, Christ stands forth.

Haworth

First through the comfortable cotton towns —
Burnley, Brierfield, Nelson, Colne — whose pubs and clubs,
Co-ops, Marks & Spencers, bingo-halls
Manumitted thousands throng, released by Saturday,
Ignoring the wayside pulpits' tattered warnings
Outside the stone-faced chapels of Dissent
That gather soot and silence with the years:

Then by road that reels about the moor,
Heaving up heights, staggering beneath
Stiff stride of pylons straight across the sky line,
Round sheep-farms crouched beside their drystone walls,
On a cool summer's evening I have come
Where the parson with the strange unYorkshire name
And delicate, pale children came, among
Booths and Ackroyds, Holroyds, Sutcliffes, Hirsts.

I park the car and get out and look round.
The museum is closed, the trippers
Have nearly all gone home: hikers and bikers,
Bright in their shirts and blouses, who have left
No sense of gaiety behind. A torn poster
Flaps on a gable-end. Dead flies
Shrivel in empty shops. It might be any
Stone-built Pennine village, struggling glumly here
To keep a lodgement underneath the moor,

Not hostile but indifferent still
To strangers, such as these were. One drank,

The others did not mix but gave no trouble.
Soon, genteel-poor and riddled with T.B.,
They guttered out like candles in a storm.
No need to gape. The place is in my bones.

But as dusk falls and a rising night-wind
Rustles the few trees, I shiver and am glad
To turn away, beckoned by lighted valleys
Whose colours flash like fairgrounds, loud with the din
Men make to frighten time, the lurker in the dark
Beyond the warmth and flicker of their fires.
Here, in spite of the guide-books, postcards
And biographies, alien, unappeased the dead
Endure in silence and the curious
Find no welcome.

Haven Street

(1)

Uncle Henry always wore his cap indoors
On top of a knitted woollen helmet which
Covered his ears and chin. He used to say his
Face was bad; and right enough it twitched at times,
Whether from neuritis or some other cause
I never knew. He had watery eyes, skin
Trout-grey, hands and nails ingrained with dirt although
They hadn't twisted warp for many a year.
And whenever father put jobs in his way
(Which he did from time to time) Uncle Henry
Used to send word his ear was bad, or turned up
Only for a day, then crept off home again,
Thin, worried, pale, to hide from draughts and nurse his
Lot, crouched by the near-dead grate, and put the blame
On Norman or MacDonald and the Tories.

(2)

Aunt Bertha was his wife, my father's sister.
Childless, they lived in a four-roomed terrace house
On Haven Street, together with Aunt Annie,
Father's other sister, who wasn't married
And always stayed at home. Somehow Aunt Bertha
Managed on their dole; patched, darned, scoured the Co-ops
For bargains, kept the place neat, sent cross-words in

Sometimes to Tit-Bits or John Bull, never won.
In old age she reminded me, with her plump
Hands, plump wrists, the dimpled smile that lit her plain
Round face, of Rembrandt's mother without the ruff.
But that of course was later. Whenever we
Visited as children (which wasn't often),
Aunt Bertha beamed at us, pressed us to bread, tinned
Salmon, tea. We pecked and shuffled, looking glum,
Yawned, the horse-hair sofa pricking our bare legs,
Daunted by dingy gaslight, their adult talk
Of small calamities among the neighbours
And cancer and T.B. Mother sympathised
As always. Father fidgeted, his restless
Mind pawing at such constraints.

                    And all the while
Aunt Annie, upright in her chair, rocked gently
To and fro, jingling her pendant ear-rings with
An air of languor and disdain. Aunt Annie,
You see, was a ruined woman. She'd demurred
When Father offered to set her up in some
Small business — dress-making, perhaps a shop. That
Would hardly have been genteel or suited to
The care and sympathy so clearly due
To one in her position. Indoors or out
Aunt Annie couldn't quite bring herself to work.
We nippers were scared of her, she seemed so grand.

(3)

After the War — my father dead, Aunt Annie
Too — my wife and I called once or twice, newly
Married. His stammer worse, Uncle Henry hid
In his corner, trying to conceal the white
Bristles that spiked his chin. Aunt Bertha, beaming,
Told us about my father as a lad — how

Mathematics hoisted him out of the mill:
How he filled a drawer with silver, kept it so
For everyone to help themselves; came home then
At all hours, whistling, up again by five. But I
Looked like my grandfather, she said — tall, thin, one
Shoulder high. She gave us some plates, her mother's
Best, unused for sixty years. Back at the flat
We rigged them up. Within a month they fell, smashed
Irretrievably. Aunt Bertha had no luck.
Then one day we heard from home that she was dead —
A fortnight later, Uncle Henry too, a
Hundred pounds in notes stuffed underneath their bed.

(4)

Sometimes now I sit in my office and I
Think of Haven Street. My carpet runs from wall
To wall; fresh flowers grace a side-table; thick
Velvet curtains reach down to the floor — the faint
Click-click of a typewriter the only noise
Obtruding through a sound-proofed door. Such timid
Gentle creatures, they waited with the patience
Of the poor, a lifetime almost, fed on scraps,
To die. And even my father lost heart at
The end — the War, his absent sons, a stroke, his
Mounting disabilities. A childless man
Whose genes lift his left shoulder, whose bloodstream bears
The family's transmissible diseases,
I pace my crumbling hereditament, scan
The entail sealed in darkness, stamped in bone; try,
Forty years too late, to make amends, piece by
Piece assembling what I find as best I can.

Reasons Of State

Mostly the butchery occurred elsewhere.
Someone was knifed among the shadows or
Garrotted at the dark turn of the stair —

A scuffle and groan, blood on the walls and floor,
Then silence. The courtiers smiled to hide their dread,
Being frightened of the truth and even more

Of being known to know. Though rumour spread
King kept his secrets, Council held their tongue
But thought it seemly they should mourn the dead

And quietly discouraged those among
The foreign embassies and fools who tried
To pry into the facts or right the wrong ...

Half-crowns paid for entry, we join the guide
Or wander round in summer frocks and flannels,
Stare at the portraits stiff with ruffs and pride,

The armour, faded tapestries, enamels.
Inside, the rooms seem cramped and dark, lit by brief
Shafts of light, revealing the dust on panels

Sprung with damp or age. Emerging with relief
We start up children's games or make for tea
At tables on a terrace, we whose chief

Virtues are domestic, who disagree
With violence, tend our gardens, knit, provide
Against the future and do not think to see

Such evil in our world. Somewhere inside
The labyrinth men shift and calculate,
Huddle together where the ways divide

Or grope and stumble through the fog of hate
(Mouths choked with dust, eyes straining) long for ease,
An end of torment, treachery, debate,

Who murder innocence beneath the trees.

Downham Revisited

Cold, witchered country this I walk today,
Seeking myself. A slim hawk hurtling there
In March's mad contention rounds to stay
And wrestle the rough wind, boisterous air
The dog snuffs, ears blown back. The brows of fells
Are vizored still with ice that blocks a slow
Spring struggling through the lanes, relieving dells
Where daffodils are shivering in snow.

Beside the church, from their long ache of bone
The dead await release, obstructed by
Millstone grit and clay compounded with limestone.
I read their names, who moulded all I see.
Perilously now rooks build; roots long dry
Stir here in earth exactly defines me.

The Farther Shore

"tendebantque manus ripae ulterioris amore"

Heysham slides past the window, once again
Materialising slowly through the dawn,
Roofs scurfed with frost, streets empty still. Here & there,
A patchwork of pink and blue beside the line,
Lights snap on in curtained bedrooms where
Men blink and rub their jowls and women yawn,
Untwining curlers. After the night at sea
I recognize my own again, this country

That I took for granted once, and thought I knew
By heart; that now, familiar and strange
Seems always out of reach when I pass through.
Again this morning as we cross the Fylde, then slow
Through Preston breakfasting in mid-December fog
And frowstiness, I search for landmarks from the train
To lead me back through my barked world, restore
The rub of its first timber and true grain.

These journeys sometimes curve into illusion, then
Swerve hard back to reality — as when
I watch old shires (sheer miracle in May)
Out of the gnarled and rooted centuries
Stubbornly flowering still, like canvas whirled away,
A stage-set in the dusk; or swinging free,
Some great cathedral ride the moon's floodtide
That lists next day, a silted argosy

Beached, barnacled with age. Such beckonings
Out of the past are tricks of light, not things
Either my father or his father knew.
Their England jolts into my view
O, on any fine Spring evening that I share
With figures in a landscape (such as, here,
Some city like a monstrous starfish stings
And thrusts its poisoned salients into)

Whom twilight has reprieved: a baby
In its father's arms, waving to the train,
Shirt-sleeved men, smoking in their allotments,
A couple strolling on a cindered lane,
Hand in hand. Or else it glimmers in the night
Through clots of steam, whisps and rags that drift
Down platforms where a few late travellers stand,
Wan faces drained of hope beneath the lamplight.

I think of them, those generations then
Entombed among the millions of men
England mangled or devoured, whose catafalques
Are these charred cities smouldering everywhere,
Incinerating time, that spout and flare
Through fissured crusts. Too late I reach
Towards lives I almost touch, they seem so near,
Yet now recede from, faster every year.

Tourist Season

Buttocks like balloons squeezed in their chairs,
Thighs plumped tight as pre-war sausages,
In bulging middle-age these burghers sit
And sweat and swill and guzzle: from Europe some,
Some from America and some
My fellow countrymen, on holiday
With false teeth and unsmiling faces.

Outside, in the white glare of midnight,
Walk the young of many nations, vaguely
Excited, hoping that something will happen;
Or they sit on the steps of public monuments.
But nobody lives here any more
And they have all come to stare at each other.

Upstairs are a dozen storeys
Of lawful embraces, snores, seductions,
Slamming of doors, flushing of lavatories,
Farts, eructations .....

If Rome was anything like this,
Do you wonder that Horace preferred his farm
And his vines and the cool Bandusian spring?

Gt. Portland Street

Caught in the undertow of memory
I am drawn back and back

And find myself again where this began
(O long ago) beneath the arc
Of lamplight like a spread-out golden fan
With faint mist thickening towards the Park
And the trains rumbling underneath my feet
And not much changed — except that no-one comes
And I am fat and bald and ridiculous.
The thing died years ago: why make this fuss?

Pale ghosts climb slowly from the Underground
In ones and twos, and go their Sunday ways
With dismal faces. A tired old crone
Under the booking-clerk's indifferent gaze
Stands clutching a sack, grateful for warmth and light.
Not much changed? I come in from the night.
It all looks shabbier now and meaner.
Shabby and mean, and shrunken in the dry, stale air
I buy my ticket and descend the stair

And gaze along the empty platform. Well,
I think I will return to my hotel
And read for half-an-hour and so to bed.
Better go quietly when all is said.
Yet I could rage with Herod, or blubber
Like a boy, to think that leper's breath
Infects her too which poisons me to death.

Pavane For the 'Forty-Five

They are shadows all, cloudy presences
Looming like mountains through the mist
By loch and sullen moor — that prince
Who thought French manners, gaiety and dash
Would fetch the burghers as they charmed the girls,
The clansmen vaunting in their pride who had
No plan but plunder, vainglory, revenge,
A cobwebbed cause which glitters briefly still,
Spangled in early dew, then snaps,
Dissolves into this rainswept desolation

Where the touring heirs of Cumberland,
Sundered here from cities, sealed
By safety-glass in coach or car
From spatterings of guilt, the stain of blood,
Fidget for the telly or The Times.

For Better For Worse

Assured of my inheritance —
Great mansion, rich demesne,
Gardens elegant, formal, trim,
The arts of Italy and France —
A lolling heir I spent my days
In idleness and wit and laughter:
For wealth and honour would come after
As summer ripened the green fruit
And you fulfilled the promise of your gaze.

In a garret now above a slum,
Arthritic fingers bent around my pen
(Those cynical remarks upon my elders!)
I scratch in vain and scratch and wonder when
In this anonymous mean place
You last showed me some favour, some
Hint of recognition. O ageing Muse,
Encumbered by an ailing poet,
Why do you thus avert your face —

To hide the ravaged glare would strike me dumb?

III

Poor Fitz

Died as he lived, an apostate; was burned
    Without the benefit of clergy,
Flowers, music, prayers one Saturday — a few
    Colleagues at hand, to do their duty.

Outside, January roared its grief,
    Lashing the graves. We filed out one by one,
Numbed in spirit, numb with cold,
    Sprinted for cars, our duty done.

Later, warmed by whisky in a snug,
    "Queer chap, old Fitz. A wasted life.
Strange that he never married. Well, lunchtime.
    Best get back home to the wife."

Next week his personal effects
    Were put away. A brisker man
Sat at his desk, despatching files
    Poor Fitz had kept, a ponderous gnome —

Big head, round belly, short, thin legs,
    The deep, slow Limerick voice —
Lumbering behind events, for ever
    Questioning that, considering this,

And making cumbrous jokes about his name
    And family's heritage and pride
That brooked no compromise. It struck me then
    He meant it all. Lived as he died

In scorn of pliant men who'd rather
      Bend than break: gave what was due
In honour forty years, took nothing back
      Except the means of holding to

His passion for astronomy. What folly
      Or madness made him fix his mind
On shadows so? — the abstract truth
      A loadstar for whose sake he dined

Always alone. O yes, a wasted life
      Compared with ours, who have promotion,
Car, kids, wife, and watch each other out of eyes
      That meeting, slide into evasion

Or signal sly complicities

The Disposition Of The Weather

My landscape turns to winter everywhere.
The seaboard stony, mountainous, is worn
By wind and rain as men are worn by time,
Bones sticking through the skin. Gaunt cliffs there,
Eyeless, towering Lears, confront the west
While the sea's hounds yelp and snarl about their feet.
By moss-grown chapels, Anglican, forlorn,
From Asia's heat the guardians rest
Of vanished empire — soldier, governor, judge.
Once upright sentinels their headstones lie
Stiffly askew: the houses they were born to,
Came home to die in and hand down,
Now carious mouths, gape at the sky.

Inland are bogs and lakes, some level pastures,
Few crops, no rich deposits in the earth.
Useless to mine or drill. There age by age
Generations wither, poverty endures —
Together man and beast inured to dearth —
Like rock beneath thin soil. And now the wind
Has settled in the east, stripping the trees
Before their time, breathing ice on pools,
Blanching field and hedgerow. A tattered thorn,
Waving its ragged arms about the sky,
Warns of the weather still in winter's horn.

One day no doubt the wind will back and veer,
Heralding rain. Brief anguish of the spring,

Blossom and leaf, will pierce the land, recalling
Lost springs elsewhere. Summer perhaps may lure
The Spanish trawlers once more with their gear
To anchor in the bay at dusk (the moth-winged,
Warm, almost Iberian dusk), their hands
Sprawled at ease on deck. And yet I know
This is the disposition of the weather,
Bleak and wild beneath all interludes; stands
Henceforth in that quarter and will moan
Wilder yet, round cape and reef, those islands where,
Their features flattened by ten centuries,
Blind saints, who never knew a temperature zone,
Gather my world into their world of stone.

Frontier Incident

That day the first rumours reached the City
Of a disaster somewhere to the north,
The wall broken, the eagles lost,
Some till then tranquil, unremembered province
Burning. But nothing changed. Trains ran to time,
Traffic filled the streets. At the airports
Visiting celebrities arrived with smiles
And statements for the waiting pressmen.
Each week-end parks and pleasure grounds were full
Of people strolling in the sun.

                    Later
Survivors appeared, in ones and twos,
A handful only, were cared for,
Found suitable jobs, but moved henceforth
Like sleep-walkers, sealed in their appalling vision.

II

Of course there were rallies, counter-attacks.
Brave men, devoted men, kept the system going,
Gave their lives in battle or at the desk.
Yet gradually dikes and frontiers crumbled,
Dock and nettle sprouted through paved streets,
Roads reverted to mud, commerce to barter,
Well-tilled land to waste.

                    While ministers at court
Bickered or wept or intrigued out of habit,

While distraught millions in the metropolis
Rushed in panic through the streets, rioting
For peace, or prayed for some miraculous
Deliverance, and bands of mercenaries,
Drunk and deserting, started to rape and loot,
The last of all the line of emperors,
Sword in hand, at a breach in the ramparts
Died, calm eyes fixed on the enemy.

To Venus
(Horace, Odes iv, 1)

Not again, O surely not again, dear lady;
I pray you, do not disturb my peace again,
Not after all these years. I am not what I was
When that cheerful girl Cynara reigned

But am getting on for fifty, after all,
And have almost forgotten the drill – those
Stern commands your lisping sons convey.
Shouldn't you be visiting love-lorn lads elsewhere?

Or, if you want to cause a proper stir,
Why not make a formal progress, swans and all,
In your full regalia, drawn by purple swans,
To the portals now of Paulus Maximus,

That brilliant young lawyer – handsome, eloquent,
Accomplished – whose clients dote on him? (They buy
His tongue but cannot buy his heart.) Your standard
He will carry far and wide, triumphing everywhere

With flutes and laughter; and by the Alban lake
He'll set your marble statue in a shrine
Of fragrant wood, and there for your delight
While clouds of incense swirl into the air

And the small pipe plays its descant to the lyre,
Fleet-footed youths and maidens twice a day

In Salian time will dance beneath the shade
And magnify your greatness in their songs.

As for me, I have no zest for contests now
Of wine or love: no longer bind my temples
With the new season's flowers or entertain
The slightest hope of a requited passion.

Then why should I be tongue-tied when she comes?
Why should her image trouble my dreams so,
Elusive phantom I pursue in vain
Among the Campus Martius' alleyways

At dusk and through the fields? If she should vanish
All will go dead within, or worse (far worse),
Empty years stretch out while underneath
The thickening crust the sterile fires still burn.

Queene And Huntresse

You define my world; bring
Into focus everything
The night obscures; reveal
The shabby shifts that make up me
And simply by being you,
So freshly minted, bright and true,
Expose the grubby counterfeit
That passes here for currency.

Glimpsed only through your cloudy veil
Pacing above, you silence all
The grunting rout in this gross sty,
Circe's swine, that kick and brawl,
Compact of envy, malice, gall,
Moon-struck now: amongst whom I,
Who stumbled on your nakedness,
Tremble for that discovery.

Perseus

Somehow it must be done. Clenched will
And muscled arm were not enough, he knew;
Such simple attributes, for all his skill
With spear and sword-blade, would not see him through.

Even with aid of gods he could not face
In hell's murk what waited for him there,
But only through obliquity of glass
Confront the writhing snakes, withstand that stare.

Must then in a sweat of horror hack
With eyes averted, slithering in blood,
Rip the dripping head-piece from the neck
And scrabble with his burden through the wood.

The exploit had its uses, he would learn,
Calm later and considering — the tale alone
Would silence disaffection, the head turn
His enemies into astonished stone.

Felt play of air, sun warm upon his skin,
As petrifaction slowly spread within.

Galatea To Pygmalion

Now my blocked mouth is loosed. My eyes
Through marble's veined opacity
Swim into light; breasts, shoulders, thighs
Break surface, rippling the stone.
Out of mute matter, clogged obstruction,
Dragged by your urgent hands I rise.

Sea-sparkle, dance of wind and sun
Among the leaves, dazzle me still.
Brine tingles on crushed lips, my tongue
Tastes the salt earth, whose each deft thing
Wounds and delights me — stumbling
Still through this bright world I venture on.

You turn away, repelled to see
Your once pure marble a botched creature,
The breached, sacked citadel so lately
Stormed by your lust. Yet I assume
Gladly what you shrink from, would disown,
Your inmost self fleshed, every flaw, in me.

Nocturne

Tangled in gantries still, a struggling moon
(That sidled over mudflats on the shore,
Slipped past sheds, fingering freight
On puddled quays) inches up the windy sky.
Now, last buses leave for depots with a roar
That dribbles into silence. Late cars
To laurelled suburbs swishing home, wink
Round corners, vanishing in spray. Now only clocks
Possess the town, leaning over roofs to pry
At lovers in their doorways, shuttered bars,
Or tall as cyclops, each with one fixed eye,
Stalk drink-befuddled sailors back to docks.

Now mind unclogged runs clear at last, emptied of
Day's clatter and the clutter of the day.
I walk the streets mobs bullocked through,
Butting and mauling in the blind affray
Of Green and Orange with their god-crazed eyes,
Despair and rage at riot in their blood,
Here, out of sight, you took your slender rise,
Through all the press and trample of the crowd
Frail and inviolate; and hidden still from view,
Past midnight now you circle somewhere home.
But look, from every wisp and whorl of cloud

The moon steps free, scouring rooftops white,
Cascading through stone chasms, silently
Flooding the fronded city with salt light.

Among the symbols of your plenitude
Through all the glittering forest spread
And coral glades, lone traveller I move,
Your incandescence blazing in my head.

Retrospect

Ares and Aphrodite snared
In fine-meshed verse: to catch these
Was to be his compensation
But the great gods broke the net with ease.

He patiently retrieved his gear
And limped away, resolved to trawl
Elsewhere for fish of rainbow hue.
Plain cod and hake: his meagre haul

Rots daily on the harbour wall.

Against Abstraction

Miles don't matter —
    By the score, few or one,
    They come to this, that you are gone.

And more than distance time
    Divides. A moment, like the Fall,
    Here or elsewhere, shatters all.

How mean these fears.
    I snatch my little good
    And hoard it from the multitude

While you, whose bounty
    Shames me so, set out
    Waving a gay good-bye to doubt,

Are lost among
    Restless millions blown around
    Like tickets on the Underground.

Unlike that girl
    Velasquez drew, of earth and fire
    So compacted that desire

In the beholder yields
    To contemplation of stillness
    Past all repose or reach of flesh

We change, but only grow
     By striking deep. Such spread
     Of leaf and blossom overhead

Declares you rooted so,
Grounded here, no matter where you go.

An Enemy

Converting your base metal into gold
Would cost me no small labour. I refrain
Partly from sloth, partly from conviction
That there are better things to do, but chiefly
Because we stand together on the same
Doomed raft, swirling into the dark.

A Narrow Place

Ieu sui Arnaut, que plor et vau cantan.

I have pinched and scraped, sulked too long
Shuffling all these grimy years among
The mean black streets and crooked alleyways
Of my constricted heart; have grubbed about
Its garbaged gutters for stale scraps
To eke my destitution out.
The dole affords a man no sense
Or expectation of magnificence.

How then could I know, how guess
That out of the squalor, smoke and mess,
The narrow ginnels, you would rise
With your soft mouth and grey-green eyes,
My phoenix-girl, and clap your wings
In joy; and by this miracle assert
Your true descent — not out of common things
But the high lineage you bear from kings?

What it devours it yet makes new
This conflagration in the dark
Of bird and bush and living tree
That as it blazes blossoms too
And sears and scorches, scouring me:
By which, with perfect clarity
Eyes long accustomed to the murk,
Undazzled, unamazed, now see.

That ruin rings this festival, I know,
But move here into settled night
My dread consumed all in delight,
Rejoicing, love, yet weeping too
That I, whose rotten makeshifts time leaks through,
Seeps within and spreads still like a stain,
Have only rags to shelter you
And keep your frail hands warm in the cold rain.

On A Recent Happy Event

That clammy toad with popped
Green stare and palpitating chin
Who squatted at table, belching, blown
So tight he could not budge

By sliminess has slithered, flopped
Into preferment: swells, a judge,
To our amazement and his own.
Ermine, wig conceal his grin

Shovelling flies and harlots in.

A Prospect Of The West

After the sudden spring, wonder of earth's waking,
Stir of wild things in the woods at dawn
About the sleeping house, all day in elms
The rooks' indignant clamour, summer failed us,
Turned wet and cool, with cloud upon the hills,
A blustery wind persisting day by day.
All we had hoped for then we somehow missed
Which others seemed to gather and enjoy;
And not the unregarded moments only —
Blue brilliance of mornings, sunlight splashed
Beneath the planes about the cobbled square —
But grace of growth and gaiety and ease,
The long, hot season nourishing the seed
That strives towards fulfilment.

                    So summer passed
Unnoticed almost till its end drew near.
We cut our sheaves, garnered the meagre harvest
And hid our disappointment from each other
In silence or in talk of other things.
Now clear weather holds before the turning world
Topples into winter. A few late bees
Fumble the fuchsias flowering still in hedgerows.
Peacock sunsets spread their purple glory,
Foundering at last like galleons on fire
Whose pennants stream at mastheads to the end.
In dews of morning after early frost
A full-formed rose gleams still; and axe-blade sharp,
Great headlands splinter the unmoving sea.

What's then to come? At evening down the lane
A whistling lad brings news of distant wars, unreal
Calamities, the cries of time-trapped men
Enacting their delirium of gall
And greed and lust. All's steady yet, no stir
Or flicker from the weather lurking here
Below earth's rim. What gusts, though, gashed,
Smashed the gull and wrung the shag's fine neck,
Honed down to bone the saints in their stone cells
Who shivered at their prayers along this coast
And groped for mercy through the gale? What terror
Did they know, what shelter find here from
That whirlwind outside time but sticks and straw?

Evensong

"he hath scattered the proud in the imagination of their hearts"

Mist-fall, leaf-fall, the plane trees flare
Like torches, showering gold: leaf-fall, dusk-fall,
Settling now to sharp October night
With streetlamps wreathed in fog
And swirl of faces under yellow light,
The confident eye, uncertain smile
Looming and vanishing.

              Now bearded youths
And foolish virgins in 'phone booths,
Lodged against the windows, grin
Down mouthpieces at unseen dates.
Women bulge with shopping bags,
Shoal in supermarkets, nibble stalls,
Nudge homeward, groceries gathered in;
And pub doors swing by dockyard gates
Spilling dunchered men and din.
The city stretches, contemplates
Its long weekend. The pleasures beckon
Of Friday night and Saturday,
Fags and booze and fornication
Which Sunday drowses, belches on.

II

Slops through the window from the street
The drumming life that roars below
And eddies down the ward. Here in neat
White rows as in a catacomb we lie
Entombed in our failed bodies. Each
Confronts alone another night
Of antiseptic smells and sweat
And whisperings by dim blue light,
Ebbed, slack hours when doubt and fear
Spread like mudbanks, looming clear
Of day's receding tide. One by one
We gather on the shore
As souls upon that stagnant reach
Who wait for the grim ferryman,
Palms black with obols, to appear.

III

Three-o-clock. Life everywhere
Contracts into its inmost keep,
Beleaguered, sapped, as out
Of hiding places cold winds creep
To occupy the town. In ragged bands
They loot the bins, whirl scraps about,
Rattle rotten windows, blow
Across the derelict decades,
Pocked, scarred wastes abandoned to the slow
Attrition of corrosive years
Where memory shoots random flares
Ripping the dark, and on the wire
The insomniac in silhouette
Twitches, mouthing, staring yet.

What treasons hidden in the blood,
Heart's abjurations, have betrayed me,
Dismembered here? — bones, hands, feet
Strewn through the city street by street
Or scattered in the river's mud
With rusty cans and old spitoons,
Crack-voiced Orpheus whose head croons
Still the perils of the night,
Unheard. Now may it drown
Under the snores, the drunken sleep
That stupifies this brawling town.

IV

But lighten at last our darkness.
As blotchy dawn with smoke-sore eyes
Peers through blinds, fumbles sheets
And underclothes on chairs, may
Mind struggle up to consciousness
Heaving the body from the crumpled bed;
And cranes like herons motionless
With lifted beaks along the shore
Strike at barges, buses, streets,
From our fragments framing day.

An Exorcism

The thick blood smokes. Fend off those shades,
That woman in her scarlet dress,
That muttering man. I would not hear them. They
Pre-figure what they cannot say.

Let others drink. See, these are froth.
A drop revives them and they fall
To cards, coquetry, scandal, snuff,
Dallying so with silken stuff

They have no time to prophesy.
Leave them be. That flesh drips down to bone
And lipless mouths no longer kiss —
Their squeaky chatter comes to this.

But that man shoulders through the throng,
Stoops at the pit, lips darkening.
Begin, begin then, since I must
Parley with your raging dust.

The mournful treacheries that roosted in
Your riven heart, like ravens in a keep,
Flap here in mine, craws crammed with carrion.
Your tale's foretold. But speak; have done.

Sea-Change

What laughter stirs him, couched
In sand and leaves, that wanderer
With salt-encrusted limbs, the sea-chafed eyes,
Who rustles like a lion in the brake
Shaking off sleep? Bursts forth —
What sack and pillage, spoil
Of cities, mangled men, confront the cool
Slim girl among her squealing handmaids? Crouched
At her feet, what cry of bone for rest
Craves parley here? For soothing oil,
Her supple hands, the knotted sinews ache.

But needle drags him north,
Tide pulls, no matter what the haven.
Slips from her arms into his element
That howls about him, homing through the night
Towards a son unfathered, an old man
Sonless, memory gone, and wan
Penelope, dozing by candlelight
Who sweats in nightmare, seeing him heave
(Those twenty stiffening years) his girth
Ashore, the bloated dead
Heaped on his back like barnacles, and weave
Segmented thighs, the bulging, hairless head,
To make a havoc of his hearth.

A Question Of Identity

I surface slowly, sink, rise, sink
Again. "He's coming round", a low
Voice says. I'm coming round then. "Who
Are you?" Three faces, indistinct,
Hover above. I try to think —
My collar's off, my shirt's undone,
Sopped in sweat — and focus on
A tablet set into the wall
Which names a benefactress. So,
That's where I am. Who am I, though?

Well, I used to be myself. I wear
My clothes, of course — that tie is mine,
This jacket too: support my wife,
Open my letters, sharp at nine
Drive to the office. You might say
I'm oiled by habit, strict routine,
Domestic, mated, middle-class,
The sort of cog worn frictionless
By use, that spins the whole machine.
Only, it's not me who leads that life.

No. Nowadays, there's wild uproar
Within. Caliban floors Prospero,
Ariel raves. All stagger, snore,
Slumped in a heap, till you restore
With syringe and needle, deft, cool hands,
A truce among my brawling glands —

As if just now I'd strayed into
The Quattrocento and you three
Were Botticelli's Graces. My
Name? My occupation? Certainly.

But you are still anonymous
In white starch, your separate selves
Doffed, bleached out, intent again
On your next patient while I fuss
With tie and collar, assembling this
My compound ghost, as best I can;
To stumble out into the rain,
Indexed, filed, on the record
In triplicate, my fissures shored —
Towards what further precipice?

Single Ticket

To a flutter of flags and handkerchiefs
We step into the huge arena,
Sacrificial victims, who wave in turn
Towards faces penned behind the barricades.

Some with foreboding watch, some with grief,
But most from curiosity, here to fill
An idle afternoon with buns and tea,
The thrill of possible disaster.

These we disappoint, climb clear and cross the coast.
Ships like slugs trail their white slime
In and out of Liverpool; and slowly clouds
Slide shut below, rolled in by the Atlantic.

We chat and smoke, cocooned in noise and comfort,
Who smell still of the miles of mouldering brick,
The millions lodged there underneath the grime —
Heading for gull-screams, granite, silence.